Heads Up!

How To Use This Book

There are lots of extras in this book aimed at helping you with writing your e-mails, letters, and resumes.

BRAIN JAM

Brain Jams offer activities to get you thinking creatively and give you a chance to hone your skills.

PROJECT JUMP START

Project Jump Starts provide that sometimes necessary extra push to get you going on your own e-mails, letters, and resumes.

TIP FILE

Tip Files offer up all sorts of helpful suggestions and hints on getting the project done.

RESOURCES   RESOURCES

These icons will lead you to more information.

ORDINARY   **EXTRAORDINARY**

Throughout the book you will see the ordinary and the extraordinary side by side. With revisions and some thought, these comparisons show you what you can accomplish.

Photographs © 2005: AP/Wide World Photos/Markus Schreiber: 108; Corbis Images/Marc Brasz: 32; Getty Images/Hans Wild/Time Life Pictures: 81; Library of Congress via SODA: 104.

Cover design: Marie O'Neill
Page design: Simon Says Design!
Cover and interior illustration by Kevin Pope.

Library of Congress Cataloging-in-Publication Data

Nobleman, Marc Tyler.
Extraordinary e-mails, letters, and resumes / by Marc Tyler Nobleman.
    p. cm — (F. W. prep)
Includes bibliographical references and index.
ISBN 0-531-16759-3 (lib. bdg.)   0-531-17575-8 (pbk.)
1. Letter writing. 2. Electronic mail messages. 3. Resumes (Employment) 4.
Cover letters. I. Title. II. Series.

PE1483.N63 2005
808.6—dc22
                                        2005010199

EXTRAORDINARY
E-mails, Letters, and Resumes

by Marc Tyler Nobleman

Franklin Watts®

A Division of Scholastic Inc.
New York • Toronto • London • Auckland • Sydney
Mexico City • New Delhi • Hong Kong
Danbury, Connecticut

EXTRAORDINARY E-MAILS, LETTERS, AND RESUMES

ASSIGNMENT:

So Why Have You Been Assigned to Write an E-mail, Letter, or Resume?

Unlike that obscure formula you learned in science class or the dates of the battles of the Revolutionary War you memorized for history class, you will be using these writing skills for the rest of your life.

Writing assignments, such as e-mails, letters, and resumes, are also a part of the plan your state has for your education. Each state in the country has its own educational curriculum plan for you and other students in your state. These plans are called educational standards. From **California** to **New York**, from **Minnesota** to **Texas**, the standards call for students to tackle a variety of written communication projects. In **California**, for instance, eleventh and twelfth graders are expected to be able to fill out job applications and create resumes. **Florida** wants students in grades nine through twelve to be able to write successfully for a variety of occasions, audiences, and purposes. **Texas** wants students to be able to write in different forms, such as memos or resumes.

E-MAIL, LETTER, or RESUME

Even if your state doesn't specifically require
writing these types of documents, who wouldn't
want to be able to create an attention-grabbing
resume or to write a persuasive letter
or e-mail?

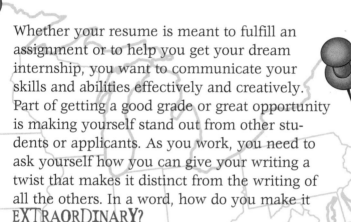

Whether your resume is meant to fulfill an
assignment or to help you get your dream
internship, you want to communicate your
skills and abilities effectively and creatively.
Part of getting a good grade or great opportunity
is making yourself stand out from other students or applicants. As you work, you need to
ask yourself how you can give your writing a
twist that makes it distinct from the writing of
all the others. In a word, how do you make it
EXTRAORDINARY?

Part of making any project EXTRAORDINARY—
whether it's an e-mail, letter, or resume—is knowing
what is expected of you and surpassing those
expectations. These projects are opportunities for
you to develop and express your own creative
ideas while developing your skills as a writer and
communicator.

There's a heatwave of memos
and resumes cropping up deep
in the heart of Texas . . .

Check Out Your State's Standards!

Want to get ahead of the game? Take a look at your state's standards for this year and the years ahead. If you're ready to check out your future, try visiting the Developing Educational Standards site at: **http://www.edstandards.org/Standards.html.** On it, you can find links to the educational departments of every state and even focus on language arts in particular.

For more of a national overview of language arts standards, here are a few of the twelve national educational standards created by the National Council of Teachers of English (NCTE). (For a complete list, visit NCTE's Web site, **http://www.ncte.org.**)

By writing e-mails, letters, and resumes, you demonstrate several key skills mentioned in the standards:

- Writing e-mails, letters, or resumes indicates that you know how to use written language to communicate effectively with a range of audiences and for different purposes.

- The creative and logical tools you use while writing an extraordinary e-mail, letter, or resume demonstrates your knowledge of writing strategies and the writing process and your ability to use them effectively.

- E-mails, letters, and resumes are examples of your knowledge of language structure, language conventions, figurative language, and genre and your ability to employ this knowledge to create texts.

Heads Up!

So Here's the Scoop

When teachers grade business documents, they use a number of factors to determine your score. This information will change from class to class and teacher to teacher, but these are the general guidelines for how your writing project will be graded.

Focus: Is it clear?

Format: Does it follow the required format?

Structure: Is the order in which the information is presented logical?

Audience: Is the document tailored appropriately to reach its intended audience?

Grammar: Are there any grammatical errors?

Punctuation: Is the document punctuated properly?

Spelling: Are there any misspelled words?

Word usage: Does the writer use lively verbs and strong vocabulary words?

Why Should I Use This Book?

Or, why lump e-mails, letters, and resumes together in one book? Each of these items is related to communication, both business and personal, and each can play a crucial role in your life. You will be called upon numerous times in your daily activities to express your thoughts clearly.

Most jobs require writing of some kind. This is true even for jobs in which people don't sit at desks all day. A mechanic might have to write a pamphlet describing his or her body shop's policy on auto repairs. A professional athlete might be asked to write a regular column for a sports magazine. A surgeon may be asked to write and give a speech on a daring new medical procedure he or she devised. In all of those scenarios and countless more, that person will want to express himself or herself well. None are full-time writers, but they should still embrace their writing task with vigor and expertise.

There are a number of different types of written correspondence, but here are the primary ones you will learn about in this book:

E-mails

Learn how to write electrifying e-mails, from casual to formal.

Personal Letters

Learn how to write a compelling personal letter for a variety of purposes.

Business Letters

Learn how to write effective business letters that impress your boss, your customers, and yourself.

Resumes

Learn how to create a resume that shows your strengths and makes you irresistible.

Writing different types of documents involves understanding the different formats and developing effective communication skills. This book will show you how to follow the proper format while filling it with extraordinary content.

Write with Might

Though this book spotlights three diverse kinds of writing, certain rules always apply to all of them:

- **Targeting counts.** Address each piece of correspondence to a name—and the right name. If you don't know who that is, call. Which letter do you think will get opened first, one addressed to Mr. Ed Juranski or one addressed to "Personnel Department"?

- **Brevity counts.** That means get to the point. Whoever is reading e-mails, letters, and resumes is busy and can't waste time on two pages when one would do. For the purposes of this book, pretend your writing is always in the "One Page or Less" lane at the correspondence supermarket.

- **Spelling counts.** The most gripping letter or the most stellar resume loses a lot of its oomph if it contains even one spelling mistake. Yes, just one. Even if it's a difficult word. Or the (long) name of a person. Any. Single. Word.

- **Vividness counts.** In other words, "show, don't tell." Don't just say you are smart. Instead, give an example of something you've done that proves it.

- **Presentation counts.** This is not about the writing itself but the package it comes in. After striving to make your sentences shimmer, don't muck them up with a splotchy print job, a reused envelope, or any other sloppiness.

Check Before You Send

Before you send out any printed piece of writing—and even important e-mails—take the following steps:

Revise. Don't send out the first draft, even if you think it's golden. Put it away for a day—or longer if you're not under time pressure—then revisit it. You'll almost definitely find passages in desperate need of a tweak. And you won't believe that you didn't notice them the first time.

Spell check. Do this in two ways: using the computer's version, then the human version (meaning yourself). Computer spell checks uncover lots of mistakes, but their are mistakes they might miss. For example, in the previous sentence, "their" should be "there," yet some spell checks might miss that because "their" is also a word—it's just used wrongly here. If you don't trust yourself, recruit someone else.

Ear check. Read your correspondence aloud, or ask someone to read it to you. Some awkward writing may not seem awkward when read silently, but it becomes obvious when you hear it. The eyes can be fooled but the ears can't!

"I love revisions. Where else in life . . . can spilled milk be turned into ice cream?"
—Katherine Paterson (1932–)

Think about your purpose before type.

Extraordinary writ
has a personality—yo

Imagine your aud
as you write.

CHAPTER 1

YOUR PERSONALITY ON PAPER

You Are What You Write

You Are What You Write

This might seem strange at first, but you are what you write. The way you commit words to paper can reveal a lot about you. The subjects you write about show what your interests are. The method in which you present your writing shows your organizational skills. The lack of mistakes in spelling, punctuation, and grammar shows your attention to detail. And the words you use and the order you put them in shows your creativity and, in most cases, your personality.

You try to make your best impression when you meet someone, whether it's a friend's parent, the new kid who just moved to town, or a stranger next to you in line at the movies. You do that mostly by what you say. **When you verbally communicate with a person, there are three different elements at work: body language, tone of voice, and words.**

In written communication, the first of those three factors—body language—isn't there at all. A writer's facial expressions and gestures don't accompany his or her words as you read them. The second factor—tone of voice—is there, but it's easy to misinterpret. Striking the right tone in your writing can be a challenge, as you will soon see (and hear).

Getting Your Message Out There—Carefully

That leaves only your words to get your message across. Now you can see why it's important to choose your words with precision. At times only one additional or omitted word—or the wrong word—can make all the difference. Look at these examples.

1 While on paper I may resemble others who have contacted you, I believe that meeting me in person will not distinguish me.

2 While on paper I may resemble others who have you, I believe that meeting me in person will distinguish me.

3 While on paper I may resemble others who have contacted you, I believe that meeting me in person will extinguish me.

The first sentence has an extra word that destroys its intentions. The second leaves out a word that makes it read kind of creepy. And the third just botches a word altogether.

While your teacher may take off a few points for these types of errors, an employer who reads any of these sentences in a cover letter for a job opening or internship might not give you a second chance. He or she would surely know you made an honest mistake, but that might be all it takes for him or her to pick someone else to come in for an interview.

Unlike spoken words, written words can stick around a while. They don't linger in the air for a moment and then fade off, like speech. Written words remain on desks until they are graded or in files waiting to be reread one day. In other words, your words are instant artifacts of the past. And you only want to leave the best behind, right?

Who Is the Recipient?

An extraordinary letter writer always considers who will be reading his or her correspondence. An e-mail to a friend about a problem with science homework will use more casual language than a letter requesting a scholarship application. You want to use a friendly, relaxed style when communicating with someone you're close to. For more formal occasions, a more serious style is called for.

Along with your intended recipient, think about your purpose. What do you hope to accomplish with this e-mail, letter, or resume? Identifying your objective will help you better organize and express your thoughts.

Great Readers Equal Great Writers

In your quest to write better, don't stop at reading this book. Samurai didn't train for only a single day before going into battle. Pilots don't test-drive one plane, then hop into the cockpit of a jumbo jet. So read a lot.

Everything you read will empower your writing, and not just books about writing. In a short story a friend wrote, you might stumble across a pleasing turn of a phrase. From a magazine article you might finally figure out what some Latin word you often see actually means. Sometimes you might not even realize what is sinking in and when. From comic books to CD reviews, from banned books to blogs, there's value in it all. Any reading is better than no reading. Good writing will inspire you. Bad writing will demonstrate what *not* to do in your own work.

GET WORD SMART

Word Menu by Stephen Glazier is an ingenious reference book that should be as well known to you as a dictionary and a thesaurus. It organizes words by subject matter. For example, if you suddenly can't think of the word for the machine people jog on indoors, flip to the Health and Fitness section and look under "Equipment." You'll see you were chasing the word "treadmill." Or if you want to use another word for "blue" but are drawing a blank, check the Colors section and take your pick, from "azure" to "zaffer."

"Many people believe letters the most personal and revealing form of communication. In them, we expect to find the charmer at his nap, slumped, open-mouthed, profoundly himself without thought for appearances. Yet, this is not quite true. Letters are above all useful as a means of expressing the ideal self; and no other method of communication is quite so good for this purpose."

—Elizabeth Hardwick (1916–)

ONLINE ASSISTANCE

Want to find a fact? Check on how to spell a word? There are a number of places for you to turn for help online:

The One Look site, **http://www.onelook.com,** searches nearly one thousand online dictionaries and encyclopedias at once. Whether you want to confirm a spelling, check a definition, or find a synonym, One Look will get the job done quickly.

Bartleby offers a host of reference books online at its site, **http://www.bartleby.com**. Here you can find *The Columbia Encyclopedia, The American Heritage® Dictionary of the English Language,* and the 1918 edition of *The Elements of Style* by William Strunk Jr.

Three Keys to Being a Better Communicator

The secret to extraordinary communication is simple: honesty (which also happens to be the best policy). If you try to come across as someone you're not, it will stand out—but not in the way you want. The reader will probably feel that the letter is phony somehow, though he or she may not be able to put a finger on why. But because of this doubt, he or she will pass you by, looking for someone who seems genuine.

What are some ways to be honest in correspondence? Here are just three.

Directness. If you state in a cover letter, "I want this job and here's why," that will capture an employer's attention. It's confident but not cocky. It starts to convince him or her that you might be a good fit, because you have passion and a reason for approaching this particular company.

Details. Cracker Jack® is known for having a prize in every box. People adore the caramel-coated popcorn and peanut snack on its own; the prize is a gem among gems. Your correspondence can follow that lead. The whole letter should be written smoothly, but slip in at least one unconventional detail about yourself that will give you an added sparkle or a memorable edge. People who read lots of e-mails or cover letters won't respond to generic language or vagueness meant to sound intellectual, but the right nugget of information about you will wedge into their minds like corn kernels in your teeth.

Dependability. Close your correspondence with a call to action—for yourself. For example, write that you'll follow up by phone in a week, and then do it. It shows you're serious. You are portraying yourself as a person who takes initiative and earns trust.

After talking for only a minute with someone you've just met, you both already have a snapshot of each other's personality. No matter how long it takes to write, the average cover letter may take less than a minute to read—and it also gives as quick a sense of the writer's personality. You don't change your personality every time you meet someone new, so why would you change your style of letter writing?

If you're optimistic in person, be optimistic on paper. If you're curious in person, be curious on paper. If you're funny in person, there are appropriate ways to let a little of that humor creep into professional correspondence.

"Everybody is original, if he tells the truth, if he speaks from himself. But it must be from his *true* self and not from the self he thinks he *should* be."
—Brenda Ueland (1891–1985)

BRAIN JAM:
A Language Warm-up

Finding the words. Write down the five words you feel best describe you. Ask a parent and a good friend to do the same about you. Compare the three lists. Do any words or concepts overlap? If so, they are probably part of the true you you'll want to represent in your correspondence.

Get a box! As you find quotations, articles, and other material for your writing, you may want to get a box or a binder to hold your possible inspirations. This way, whenever you need a little extra help creating attention-grabbing materials, you can look at what caught your eye. Newspaper and magazine articles, advisements, quotations, and fascinating facts are all potential sparks for your correspondence.

A signature that
includes your vital
information

A polite
greeting

**CREATING EXCELLENT
E-MAIL**

The "E"
Doesn't stand
for "Easy
Way Out"

Creating Excellent E-mail

An e-mail is a letter sent at light speed, or so it seems. Electronic mail has radically changed the way people contact one another. It is a great equalizer. It allows widespread communication between people who otherwise may not be in touch by any other means. Some people know each other exclusively through e-mail and have never met in person or even heard each other's voices on the phone.

Your teachers may allow you to e-mail them to ask questions about assignments, and they may even give you an assignment requiring you to e-mail others. For example, if you're writing a paper on the history of shopping malls, you may want to e-mail the author of a new book about that very subject. Whether you're writing to your teacher whom you see every day or a person you've never met, make your e-mail extraordinary.

TIP FILE

Every part of your e-mail sends a message, including your e-mail address. Choose it wisely if you want people to take you seriously. Try using your own name instead of the name of your favorite band or sports team.

A good e-mail may have all the right ingredients but not necessarily the highest quality ingredients. A good subject line is read, while an extraordinary one is read and remembered. A good message prompts the recipient to respond at some point, while an extraordinary one entices the recipient into responding right away. A good signature tells the recipient your name, while an extraordinary one tells him or her just a little more, which is just enough to make you more interesting.

Remember, e-mail is not necessarily confidential. Any e-mail message can be forwarded to people you don't know or posted online without your approval or knowledge, even if it's marked confidential. Plus, some schools and companies screen all the mail sent and received from their building. Before you send any messages, especially sensitive ones, take a few seconds to reread your words. If you've written anything that could embarrass you if it passed in front of the wrong eyes or anything that has a good chance of embarrassing or angering someone, take it out.

Formatting Your E-mail

Most of us learn how to format a letter at some point in our school careers. A formal e-mail also needs to look a certain way. In other words, you have an obligation to make your e-mail pretty—but pretty by Web standards. Don't worry that you won't appear creative. It's not the look of your e-mail that will be extraordinary; it's the way you write it.

Type in a standard font (Arial is best) **and a standard font size** (10 or 12) for your e-mails. Skip any fancy formatting, such as colored fonts and backgrounds. Don't write in ALL CAPS. It's okay to use all capital letters for an occasional word or phrase, but never a whole e-mail or subject line. Online, it's perceived as shouting.

Use proper grammar and punctuation, even if the person with whom you're corresponding doesn't. This includes skipping Internet abbreviations such as BTW (by the way) and TTYL (talk to you later), as well as emoticons such as smiley faces. Also, go easy on the exclamation points. One is usually more than enough.

E-mail Component: "To" Line

Double-check that you have the correct addressee(s) in the "To" line. Otherwise, you may not know your message never arrived. Some computer systems bounce e-mails with incorrect addresses back to you, but others don't.

Remember, most e-mail software provides an address book. Use it. Yes, it takes time to enter in the addresses of your family, friends, and teachers, but it's worth it. You'll save time in the long run, and you'll eliminate the chance of mistyping someone's address.

LEARN SOME MANNERS

Check out *E-Mail Etiquette: Do's, Don'ts, and Disaster Tales* from *People Magazine's Internet Manners Expert* by Samantha Miller. This book of advice on netiquette is lighthearted yet practical and includes a section geared toward young people.

TIP FILE

Save templates of form e-mails—e-mails with a purpose that you'll use again.

E-mail Component: Subject Line

Some people insist that the first line of a traditional letter is the most important because it either hooks a reader or it doesn't. In an e-mail, the subject line is arguably the most important. If someone reads an enticing subject line, he or she will probably read the e-mail right away. If he or she reads a vague or dull subject line, he or she may ignore the e-mail for the time being or even delete it, if he or she doesn't recognize the sender.

Your subject line is only one line, but that one line should be all of the following:

- **Short.** Don't write an entire sentence or a long phrase all the way across the field.

- **Strategic.** Some spam filters will quarantine e-mails with certain words in the subject lines. You can't predict what all of those words are, but you can determine what some are based on the spam you yourself get. Be as specific as possible. Aside from being boring, subject lines such as "Thanks" or "Hi" may appear to be spam, too. Never leave the subject line blank.

- **Enticing** (if appropriate). Think of a subject line like a tag line on a movie poster. Those tag lines are designed to get you curious about the movie. You want a subject line that makes the recipient curious about the message that follows.

Sample Subject Lines

If you're responding to an ad for an internship or a job, the employer might specify that applicants include the job title code in the subject line. If not, use the subject line to link yourself to the available job. For example, if you're applying for a job at a clothing store, you could try the following:

ORDINARY	EXTRAORDINARY
Six years' experience in fashion industry	Will sell the shirts off your racks

Here are a few other examples for you to check out:

Ordinary Subject Line	Extraordinary Subject Line	Why It's Better
Next step	Next step—rehearse our group presentation	specifies the next step
Information you requested	Hi Barbara—bake sale statistics	doesn't read like spam; mentions addressee by name; specifies the information included
I found your name online by searching "cartoonists." Would you do caricatures at a children's birthday party?	Seeking cartoonist for children's party	doesn't use seventeen words when five will do; starts with a verb and states a need
Quick question	4-second question	not bland; catches the eye by using 4 rather than a more "rounded" number such as 5 or 10; both versions show respect for the recipient's time, but the second one is more inventive about it

E-mail Components:
The Greeting and Body

An extraordinary e-mail is direct, succinct, and if appropriate, sprinkled with a pinch of humor or an otherwise memorable line. Adhere to these guidelines as you write, and you'll notice that people will be more likely to respond.

Respect the recipient's time when composing e-mail; keep in mind who will be reading it and how. These days, many people scan their e-mails on the tiny screens of personal digital assistants like BlackBerries™ and Palms™. They'll be grateful if they don't need to scroll down much. The average business letter is a page or less, and the average e-mail should fit within one screen. So make all paragraphs—and the overall length of your message—short. Whenever possible, keep every e-mail focused on one topic. Piling on too many questions can overwhelm the recipient.

TIP FILE

Look at any messages from friends that bothered you somehow—even if it wasn't intentional. You're looking for a note or an e-mail that made you say to yourself, "I'm sure he didn't mean it that way." Sometimes people use words in a manner that would be friendly if spoken, but seem abrupt in writing. If you find one, reread it. Does it still rub you the wrong way, or can you now see that your friend didn't mean to offend you?

Some e-mail conventions are the same as the ones to use when writing traditional letters. If you're writing an e-mail to a person you don't know, address him or her as "Mr." or "Ms." (not Mrs. or Miss). With e-mail, convenience does not equal informality. **Write the e-mail as if you were speaking in person or on the phone.** This means being civil. Always say "please" and "thank you." Even people who are unfailingly respectful in person sometimes neglect these important phrases in e-mail without realizing it. But that oversight can leave an e-mail seeming rude.

Though what you write is what will distinguish your e-mail as extraordinary, when you send it is also important. **Make the effort to respond within forty-eight hours to every legitimate message you receive.** Not doing so sends a message that you're not interested or don't care. Responding will often take less time than you think it will. A one-line response, if written courteously, is often more than enough. If the issue is too complicated for an immediate answer, at least send a line acknowledging receipt and saying when you expect to get back to the sender.

"I try to leave out the parts that people skip."

—Elmore Leonard (1925–)

Other E-mail Essentials

There are a few more things to keep in mind when writing e-mails.

If you're e-mailing an important question, make it either the only line or the last line. You want it to stand out, and questions buried within paragraphs or at the top of a message are sometimes overlooked.

After you ask the question, don't bother tacking on "Please let me know" or something like it. By asking a question, it's obvious you will be waiting for an answer. Putting anything after it can act like a barrier between the question and the answer. It may sound strange, but a question followed by a statement is often left unanswered.

If you can control it, adjust your e-mail program's settings to keep all earlier messages in an e-mail thread. That way neither you nor the recipient will be left confused if you don't remember what the other is referring to. Just scroll down and check.

Similarly, strive to make each message stand alone. For example, say a friend you're partnered with for a science project e-mails you this: "Do you need more leaf samples from deciduous trees? Or coniferous?" If you need only coniferous leaves, you might write "Yes." But that could be confusing to your buddy. Better to clarify it this way: "More coniferous leaves, please. I don't need deciduous."

If you're contacting someone for the first time in a while, remind him or her who you are. This can include pasting any relevant portions of his or her previous e-mail(s) to you below your signature to refresh his or her memory.

E-mail Component: Signature

A signature is a short block of information at the bottom of each message. E-mail software usually gives you the option of setting a default signature—one that appears automatically whenever you create a new e-mail message. When you work for a company, you want to have a more professional-looking signature. A professional signature typically includes your full name, title, company name and address, e-mail address, phone number, and company Web site.

Sometimes business professionals close their signature with a line of marketing copy to do one of the following:

- introduce a new product

- promote an upcoming event

- announce an award won

- quote someone involved with the company or industry

Include a signature with every initial e-mail. (You can opt not to include it for additional e-mails in the same thread.)

E-MAIL ADVICE

Unsure of what to write in that e-mail? The career planning section of About.com has a special section on e-mail. Visit **http://careerplanning.about.com/od/communication/a/email_etiquette.htm** and check out the bounty of tips from expert guides about writing effective e-mails.

Purdue University's Online Writing Lab also offers some pointers in its handout on e-mail, which can be found at **http://owl.english.purdue.edu/handouts/pw/p_emailett.html.**

Sample Signatures for Business E-mails

ORDINARY	EXTRAORDINARY
We know what you like.	We know how discriminating you are about what products you buy. We're the same about what products we sell.
Made you smile!	Turning smiles into laughs since 1990
"I love your store!" —a customer	"Whenever I go to the mall, your store is always the first I head to!" —customer Naomi R., Redwood, SD

TIP FILE

Resist the temptation to include anything besides essential information in your signature—no risqué humor (someone may not find it funny), no long text such as lists or article excerpts, and definitely no images. All of these things increase the size of your message. Some recipients may have a limited amount of e-mail storage space or may use software that doesn't display pictures.

Sample Business E-mail with Signature Line

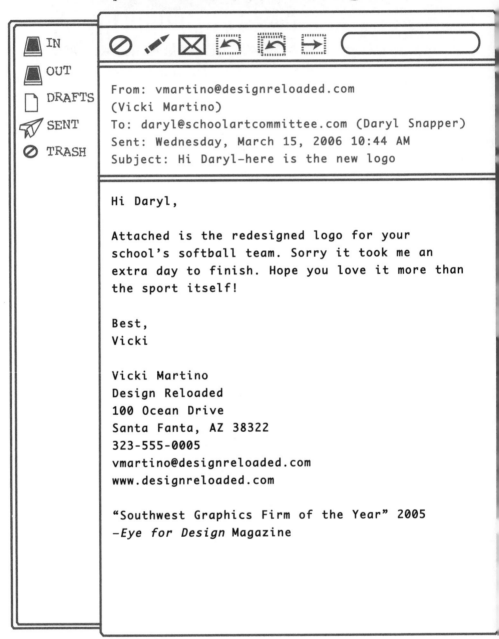

From: vmartino@designreloaded.com
(Vicki Martino)
To: daryl@schoolartcommittee.com (Daryl Snapper)
Sent: Wednesday, March 15, 2006 10:44 AM
Subject: Hi Daryl—here is the new logo

Hi Daryl,

Attached is the redesigned logo for your school's softball team. Sorry it took me an extra day to finish. Hope you love it more than the sport itself!

Best,
Vicki

Vicki Martino
Design Reloaded
100 Ocean Drive
Santa Fanta, AZ 38322
323-555-0005
vmartino@designreloaded.com
www.designreloaded.com

"Southwest Graphics Firm of the Year" 2005
—*Eye for Design* Magazine

Knowing Your Netiquette

Being extraordinary with e-mail doesn't end once you send one. You also need to know what to do next.

Following Up

If someone hasn't responded to your e-mail, use your best judgment to gauge how soon you should follow up. For an urgent matter, that might be within a week or even a day. Don't ask whether the recipient got your last e-mail. Instead, just resend the original e-mail or a one-line e-mail repeating your main question.

Copying and Forwarding

There are two ways to copy people on e-mail—regular and blind. Regular means that everyone can see everyone else's address on the recipient list. Blind means they can't. Don't abuse either function. It's considered good e-manners to copy only those people who need to know. Don't be one of those people who regularly has a fat list of addresses underneath the "To" line. It doesn't look professional, and it is a violation of privacy. You're distributing addresses whose owners may not want shared. And if you respond to a broadcast e-mail (one that goes out to a group), don't reply to all unless your comment pertains to all. When it comes to e-mail, few things are more annoying than being copied on a message that has nothing to do with you.

Use the same common sense with forwarding as you do with copying. Of course, **never forward anything confidential,** especially outside of your school, organization, or company. And you probably know this by now, but never forward chain letters of any kind. They are all hoaxes!

PROJECT JUMP START

E-mail a company for information for a school assignment or for your own interests. Remember, however, that some companies are inundated with e-mails. Some answer every one, while others are not so diligent. But write an extraordinary e-mail, and you raise your chances of hearing back.

Survey your friends. Compose an e-mail questionnaire on a subject of your choice and send a broadcast e-mail (using blind cc) to your friends. See how many respond (everyone? 50 percent? no one?). The topic can be anything from their experience with college applications to their reactions to recent movies. Regardless of the topic, make the last question as follows: "Why did you respond to this e-mail?" You'll see if it was your subject line, the first line of the body, the fact that you wrote it, or something else.

E-mail a celebrity. See which of your favorites has an official Web site. You won't be able to e-mail the star directly, but many sites do have an e-mail contact, such as the Web master. Even C-level celebs probably get too much e-mail to respond to, but challenge yourself to write an e-mail so sincere that you just might hear back. Make your compliment specific. If you have a question, ask it with such charm that it begs to be answered.

BRAIN JAM:
Explore Your E-mail

Avoid having your messages mistaken for spam.
Spam is unwanted e-mail. If you have a spam filter that
quarantines spam e-mails, do a quick survey of them.
Write down the words you see recurring in the subject
lines. This will include many words you would never use
anyway, but also some that may seem harmless, such
as cash, deal, degree, and help. Try to avoid using the
most common words that appear in spam e-mails in your
subject lines.

Look for examples of signature marketing lines.
You may discover some in your e-mail in-box, but
also consider marketing pitches in magazines and in
commercials. Then, taking inspiration from what you
find and pretending you work in your favorite industry,
write a list of three different marketing lines you could
use as your signature in a business e-mail.

An appropriate gree

A short, attention
grabbing openi
paragra

short closing paragrap

An appro

WRITING POWERFUL PERSONAL LETTERS

Snail Mail Still Works!

Writing Powerful Personal Letters

Even if most of your correspondence right now is done via e-mail, you should still know how to write a proper paper letter as well.

In fact, there still are circumstances for which writing a traditional letter will be mandatory, even though e-mail may seem much more convenient to you. For example, you may get assigned a project for which you must write a letter to a local politician to suggest a change in town or city government. Also, some companies will not process complaints submitted by phone or e-mail (and certainly not in person!). All complaints must come to them in writing by postal mail.

Five Questions Every Letter Should Answer

Like a newspaper article, a letter must answer these five questions:

- who?
- what?
- where?
- when?
- why?

Depending on the situation, a letter will also address "how." Generally, the earlier a letter answers the first five questions, the easier it will be to understand. However, you don't need to address the questions in a particular order.

Letter Format

The way you format your personal letters will vary depending on the type, but there are certain standards for most letters. Use personal letterhead or stationery so your name and return address are already printed.

BASIC PERSONAL LETTER BLUEPRINT

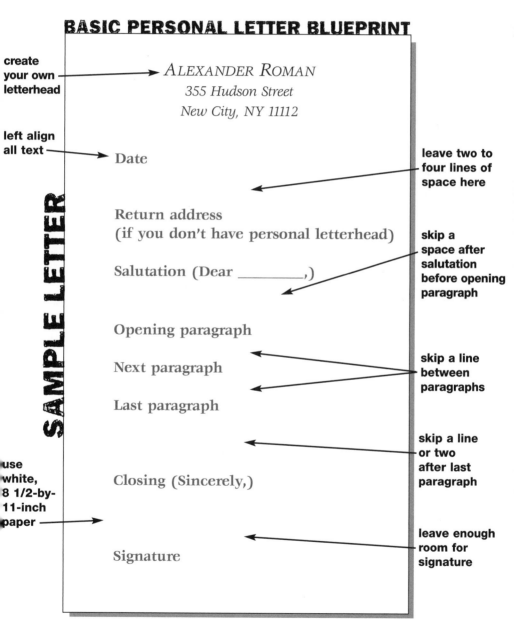

create your own letterhead

ALEXANDER ROMAN
355 Hudson Street
New City, NY 11112

left align all text

Date

leave two to four lines of space here

Return address
(if you don't have personal letterhead)

skip a space after salutation before opening paragraph

Salutation (Dear _____,)

Opening paragraph

Next paragraph

skip a line between paragraphs

Last paragraph

skip a line or two after last paragraph

Closing (Sincerely,)

use white, 8 1/2-by-11-inch paper

Signature

leave enough room for signature

SAMPLE LETTER

Here's an ordinary letter written to people who live in a condominium complex.

ORDINARY **PERSONAL LETTER**

SAMPLE LETTER

Magic Meadows Condo Association
32 Magic Meadows
Hilldale, CA 55555

May 5, 2006

Dear Magic Meadows Residents,

Many of you have expressed concern about the location in which the new pool will be built. The Condo Association would like to discuss this with you. Please join us for an open meeting on Sunday, November 2, in the Citizen Center lobby. Our objective is to choose the safest, most convenient spot we can.

forgot to include the time

We look forward to seeing you there.

Sincerely,

Michelle Ledan
CA President

Here's an extraordinary rewrite.

EXTRAORDINARY PERSONAL LETTER

Magic Meadows Condo Association
32 Magic Meadows
Hilldale, CA 55555

May 5, 2006

Dear Magic Meadows Swimmers,

As you know, the Condo Association has been
discussing where within the complex to build
our new pool. Since none of you volunteered
your living rooms, we are left with outdoor
locations only.

**humor
helps**

But we're still undecided. Please help us reach a
decision by attending our next association meeting
on Sunday, November 2, in the Citizen Center
lobby, at 1:00 P.M. All residents are welcome, even
those who prefer the ocean.

**provide
all
essential
info**

We look forward to choosing a pool location
that is best for our community.

Thank you,

Michelle Ledan
CA President

45

Thank-You Letter for a Gift or a Nice Gesture

A thank-you letter acknowledges someone's generosity, and you should write one after every gift or nice gesture that comes your way. An ordinary thank you is generic—it could be for any gift. Also, ordinary thank-you letters may read as emotionless. When the writer doesn't make the effort to write a heartfelt note, it sends a message to the recipient that the writer considered it a chore to write the note. An extraordinary thank-you letter mentions the gift or gesture specifically and spells out why you appreciate it.

Try to be sincere when penning a thank-you note for a gift. It's a straightforward task if you love the gift. It's an exercise in diplomacy if you don't. There are any number of phrases to use in a thank-you note for an unwanted gift without lying or hurting the giver's feelings. Look at the examples on the opposite page. The ordinary ones try to be cute but may insult someone. The extraordinary ones manage to sound good without being too specific.

Saying Thank You!

ORDINARY	EXTRAORDINARY
Thank you for the gift, but next time, you really don't have to get me one.	I'm flattered you thought of me.
I like your clever thinking in choosing my gift. I'll have to use some of my own to figure out what to do with it.	I should've known you would give the most unique gift!
Your gift has made history— the first polka-dotted lampshade I've owned.	It really could go in any room in our house.

Ready to say "thank you"? Here are some suggestions to follow.

Send one for any gift you receive, no matter the occasion or the size of the gift. Also send one after somebody does you a favor or a kind act that goes beyond the everyday call of friendship, such as helping you move or referring you for an internship opening.

Handwrite it on a simple card. Skip the cards with preprinted sentiments. Your own words will be much more meaningful.

Specify why you like the gift or how you will use it.

Send the letter as soon as possible after receiving the gift.

Strike the right balance between respect and familiarity.
Address the recipient by title if it's someone you don't
know or someone older. If you're writing to a friend, use
his or her first name.

Don't exaggerate. Claiming the gift is the best one
you've ever received will probably seem phony to the
reader.

Here's a sample gift thank-you letter.

EXTRAORDINARY THANK-YOU LETTER

SAMPLE LETTER

Dear Mr. and Mrs. Sprang,

As the parents of my best friend, you
know me as well as your own son. I was
beaming when I received the bookstore gift
certificate you gave me for my birthday.
The list of books and graphic novels I want
to read is getting out of hand, and this will
help me put a dent in it–plus give my library
card a rest for a change. I'll cut you a
deal–when I'm done reading each book,
I'll pass it on to Luke. This is a gift that
will keep on giving for both of us! Thank
you so much for thinking of me and for
your generosity.

Sincerely,

Jeff

Complaint Letters

A complaint letter is typically written to a company to explain your dissatisfaction with one of its products or services. **Ordinary complaint letters are whiny or aggressive. Extraordinary complaint letters sensibly state why you're unhappy and then suggest a reasonable solution.** The catch to writing an extraordinary complaint letter is that it shouldn't sound like you're actually complaining. You want to sound like you're trusting a company to fix a problem.

When writing a complaint letter to a company about a defective or unsatisfactory product or service, be diplomatic in every line. Express your frustration but in a constructive way. There is a way to be peeved and polite at the same time. You're not complaining just to get it out of your system—you're asking the company to repair or replace something. Even if the company sold a faulty product or did not keep a promise, you'll have better luck getting it to see your side of the situation if you use tact at all times.

Be mindful of your word choice. For example, which letter excerpt sounds less accusatory?

1. On March 3, Henry in your customer service department said he would send my refund check that day. It's now March 24, and he still hasn't sent it.

2. On March 3, Henry in your customer service department said he would send my refund check that day. It's now March 24, and I still haven't received it.

The second excerpt is the better way to phrase this. Sure, the writer is annoyed, and it's human to assume that he or she hasn't gotten the check because Henry has not yet sent it. However, there are other reasons a check doesn't arrive when expected—it was sent to the wrong address and was returned to the sender, or it really did get lost in the mail, to name two. Therefore, use language that gives the company the benefit of the doubt.

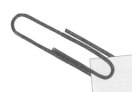

TIP FILE

Don't forget to include your contact information. Make sure that at least your name, phone, and e-mail are on everything you send out. This is a wise policy even for pages 2 and up in multiple-page documents, because pages sometimes get separated.

Be a Diplomat!

Look for ways to be diplomatic instead of confrontational. It's similar to the way people typically respond better to talking than to yelling.

Note the difference between a confrontational and a diplomatic tone.

ORDINARY confrontational	EXTRAORDINARY diplomatic
If I had known what a lousy job you would do, I never would have spent so much money on your service.	I paid a premium to get quality service, and I'm sure you would agree that a customer should get exactly what she pays for.
When I back out of my driveway, I'm unable to avoid hitting several large potholes on the street in front of our house. Please fix them this week, or else you will have to pay for the damage to my car.	For the safety of my family and everyone else who drives on Main Street, I ask you to make it a priority to fix the potholes here.
Your installation guy messed up the hookup of our washing machine, causing it to wash my delicate sweaters in hot water instead of cold. Trust me, they're completely destroyed, and I hold you responsible. I am expecting a check for $291 by the end of the week.	We recently bought a washing machine from your store and appreciated the free installation. However, we discovered after our first wash that the cold and hot water valves were reversed, which you've since fixed. This ruined $291 worth of our sweaters, for which we've enclosed copies of receipts. We hope you will see fit to reimburse us for this loss.

An Effective Complaint Letter

At the beginning explain the annoyance you're facing in a courteous tone.

If possible, **find something about the company or product to compliment.** Show that you believe in the company and like the product, if you indeed do.

Stick to the facts. State what has gone wrong, not how you feel about what has gone wrong. (Facts alone are enough to show why you're displeased.) If a company did not keep a promise or live up to a guarantee, specify that.

State how the problem has affected you negatively. Has it wasted your time? Has it hurt you or damaged your property?

In the final paragraph state your ideal solution. What will it take to make you a happy customer again? Do you want a refund, a replacement product, or something else?

If applicable, **give a date by which you expect a response.** This indicates you feel entitled to prompt action to make up for the inconvenience you've experienced.

On the right is a sample complaint letter, sent after the writer spoke with the recipient on the phone to explain the situation. You'll see that the writer nonetheless repeats her problem in writing to be sure the recipient understands it.

F. WATTS
102 UPTOWN AVENUE #119
ST. LEWIS, ME 49994

October 2, 2006

Ralph Everisto
Repair Department
Syon Electronics
88 Flag Street
St. Lewis, ME 49994

Dear Mr. Everisto:

As we discussed on the phone today, enclosed is a portable CD player that I purchased at Better Buy on 5/16/06. A copy of the receipt for that purchase is also enclosed.

use courteous tone

Approximately one month after my purchase, the device began to malfunction. When a CD is being played, the device frequently skips. Also, on three occasions in the last week alone, it got stuck in one position, causing a scratchy noise.

stick to the facts

I follow your printed instructions whenever I use the device. I have not dropped it or otherwise damaged it. It has been in my possession since I purchased it, and no one else has used it. For these reasons, I am inclined to believe that the device was manufactured improperly.

Of the four Syon products I own, this is the only one that has ever had a problem. Since I am happy with my other Syon products, I am confident that this is an isolated problem.

say something positive

Therefore, please repair or replace this unit, and send it to me at the address above. Otherwise, I would like a full refund for $49.88, the amount shown on the enclosed receipt.

Thank you for your prompt attention to this matter.

Sincerely,

F. Watts

Apology Letters

Ordinary apologies can seem forced or even insincere. Extraordinary apologies seem genuine and explain to a person who has been hurt not only that you are sorry but why you are sorry. By the time a recipient finishes reading your extraordinary apology, all is good in the world again, at least between you two.

Apologizing in writing is not a substitute for apologizing in person if the situation calls for that, but it's a classy gesture nonetheless. And since you don't have the pressure of standing before the person you've wronged, you can take the time to compose your words with care.

Incidentally, these are called apology letters, not ask-for-forgiveness letters. When you apologize, you accept responsibility for your actions. When you ask for forgiveness, you're placing a burden on someone else to act. Just apologize and hope for forgiveness.

Here's how to write a genuine apology letter.

Lead with the all-important phrase "I'm sorry." And don't dress it up—just come right out with it. You want the recipient to know without doubt that you regret what you did.

Humor is a wondrous tension reliever. Use it if you are close with the person and the situation allows for it.

Give the recipient space, and don't rush him or her. An apology with expectations is not really an apology.

End on a positive, supportive note.

Here's a sample apology.

EXTRAORDINARY APOLOGY LETTER

Dear Amy,

I am sorry I left the back door open
when I came over to your house last weekend.
For some reason, I thought we would be going
right back out. Then when we didn't, I totally
forgot I had done that. I can assure you I
won't ever do it again.

I'm just so glad Brownie wasn't missing
for long, though I know it felt long while it
was happening. The fact that she came back
in less than an hour proves how much your
cat loves you.

I understand if you're still angry at me.
But please know how much I appreciate our
friendship. To me, a true friend is someone
you can tell anything to, and that's what we've
always done with each other. When you're
ready, I look forward to picking up where we
left off.

Love,

Molly

Condolence Letters

When someone in your life has lost someone in his or her life, it is customary to send a short note that expresses sympathy. Many people are anxious about writing to someone about a person who has died. They worry that they won't be able to summon the right words.

But a condolence letter doesn't need to be moving, and it certainly doesn't need to be long. Sometimes "I'm sorry about your loss" is all that is necessary. The letter just needs to say that you're thinking about the person who is grieving, and you're remembering the person who has passed away. (Yet you should still send a condolence letter even if you did not know the person who died.)

A condolence letter should be handwritten on a plain note card. Send it as soon as you hear about the death. That's probably when the person is most in need of support.

Here are a few things to keep in mind as you start to write.

Mention the person who died by name or by the way you knew him or her. For example, if you're writing to a friend whose grandmother has passed away, you may refer to her as "your grandmother."

If you knew the person personally, **share a fond memory** so the letter might make the recipient smile.

Offer to help during the grieving process. It may just be providing an ear to listen or a shoulder to cry on.

Don't tell the recipient how to mourn by writing "Look at the bright side" or anything like that. People need to mourn in their own way and at their own pace.

Here's a sample condolence letter.

EXTRAORDINARY CONDOLENCE LETTER

Dear Ray,

My deepest condolences on the loss of your grandmother. I'll never forget all the times we went to your house after school when she greeted us with a piping-hot plate of freshly baked brownies. She always helped us get through our homework sessions deliciously.

I wish you and your family strength at this difficult time. If there's anything at all I can do, please let me know.

Your friend,

Janet

PROJECT JUMP START

 Write a friend. Craft a cheer-up or thinking-of-you letter to a friend you haven't talked to in a while. You can write just to say hi!

 Write a letter to an editor. Choose an issue that affects your school or community and about which you have an opinion. For example, do you think your town should build a youth center? Do you agree that dogs should be allowed into stores if they're on leashes? Decide where you want to send that letter— your school newspaper, your town newspaper, a local magazine, or more than one of those. If your issue is large enough, you can even send your letter to a national magazine. And if your topic is timely—and you've written about it extraordinarily—you may see it in print.

BRAIN JAM:
Get Personal!

Write a letter to yourself. This is a good way to practice letter-writing because it takes away the pressure of having someone else reading your work. Tell a gripping story that happened to you, describe a recent school assignment you liked, or analyze a job interview you went on. It may feel silly, but remember, it's just between you and you. (Mailing it to yourself is optional.)

Write an unexpected thank-you note. Think of someone who deserves thanks but may not get it often—an unsung hero, as they say. Perhaps you can write to a security guard at your school, your letter carrier, or, of course, a teacher. Saying thanks in person is one thing, but taking the time to write something can have an even more touching effect.

Get specific about complaints. Have you ever dealt with a company that you feel was unprofessional in some way? If so, plot out how you would write it a complaint letter. Ask yourself the questions below, and then answer them. Those answers will be the framework for your letter.

- What is unsatisfactory about this company's product or service?

- Did I ask the company for help but not receive it?

- What is my goal in writing a complaint letter to the company? What would I like it to do for me?

short attention-gr
opening paragraph

accurate recipi
name and addre

short closing pa

cordial sign-off

clear messa
written wit

CHAPTER 4

CRAFTING DYNAMIC BUSINESS LETTERS

Putting Your Letters to Work

Crafting Dynamic Business Letters

Many high-school students write their first business letters long before they enter the business world. Remember, a business letter takes many forms. You may be selling something in your community, such as a bicycle, and you'll write a sales pitch for your flyer. You may be selling yourself in a cover letter when applying for an after-school job. You may be assigned to pair up with another student to write letters of recommendation about each other, as if you were both applying for your dream jobs.

Cover Letters: The Basics

Most correspondence you send will include or consist entirely of a cover letter. For example, you may need to write one when you apply for a scholarship. Perhaps the term "cover letter" diminishes its importance. It's not merely a cover of something else, it's significant in its own right. Typically, you'll send a cover letter and a resume when applying for any job or internship—even if an employer requests only a resume. A cover letter is a warm way to introduce yourself, and it can put forth information about you that a resume usually doesn't, such as the following:

- Your letter-writing skill

- Your career objective (if it is not on your resume)

- Your reason for approaching a particular company

- Your salary history and/or requirements

- Your manners

BASIC BUSINESS LETTER BLUEPRINT

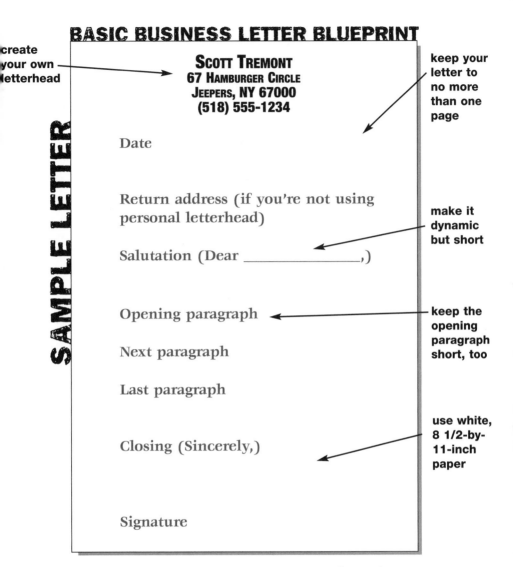

create your own letterhead

SCOTT TREMONT
67 HAMBURGER CIRCLE
JEEPERS, NY 67000
(518) 555-1234

keep your letter to no more than one page

SAMPLE LETTER

Date

Return address (if you're not using personal letterhead)

make it dynamic but short

Salutation (Dear _____,)

Opening paragraph

keep the opening paragraph short, too

Next paragraph

Last paragraph

use white, 8 1/2-by-11-inch paper

Closing (Sincerely,)

Signature

If your cover letter accompanies a resume, keep the paper you use for both documents consistent, and match your letter to the font style and size of the dominant font on your resume. You want your letter to look professional, so keep it clean.

Address your cover letter to a name, not to "Sir," "Madam," "Dude," and so on. An exception is if you're responding to an advertisement in which no name is provided; otherwise call the company and ask to whom you should send the cover letter and resume.

If you're given a name that could be male or female, such as Chris or Terry, ask which it is. Also include the person's title: Mr., Ms., Dr., Emperor, and so on. If there's no way to obtain a name, try something heartier than "To whom it may concern," such as "Good morning."

If you can locate a name, **double-check the spelling of that name and the name and punctuation of the company.** If the company is called Newz U Can Use!, make sure you haven't written the less dramatic— though more grammatical—News You Can Use. When proofreading your letter, be on the lookout for names with more than one spelling, like Marc/Mark or Catherine/Kathryn/Katherine.

Keep each paragraph short. In general, a cover letter has three or four paragraphs, and the longest is the middle one (or one of the middle two). The shortest is the last, though the first can also be short for dramatic effect. In cover letters for internships or jobs, don't waste precious space by repeating information that is on your resume. A resume summarizes what you've done in the past. A cover letter proclaims what you can do in the future. And always be personable, but don't get too chummy. It's a business letter.

"It helps to have an imaginary listener when you are writing . . . so that you will be interesting and convincing throughout. . . . You have to hold your audience in writing to the very end—much more than in talking, when people have to be polite and listen to you."
—Brenda Ueland (1891–1985)

Avoid the following:

- clichés and other empty phrases—
  no "people person," "leadership qualities,"
  and so on

- slang

- abbreviations, even in your contact information;
  for example, write out "Avenue," "Street," or
  wherever you live

- contractions (optional but often recommended;
  use your judgment depending on how formal
  the industry you're applying to is)

Ask somebody to read every important letter you send out; if no one is available, read it aloud so your ears might catch errors your eyes missed.

The average employer scans a cover letter in twenty to thirty seconds. That may seem fast, but it's plenty of time to WOW them if you choose your words with conviction.

Mailing It Out

Send cover letters and resumes in a catalog-size envelope rather than a standard #10 envelope. This means you won't have to fold them to mail them, and employers won't have to unfold them to read them. It may be a tiny difference, but your materials will seem a smidgen more appealing if they don't have crease lines in them.

Also, there's some human psychology involved. Some people subconsciously open mail from easiest to hardest (relatively speaking). To busy people, opening a flap and sliding out the contents is quicker than—and therefore preferable to—opening a flap, pulling out the contents, and unfolding them. It may mean you're making your first impression before many others.

LOSE THOSE CLICHÉS

If you write a phrase you've heard before, it's probably a cliché, but check out *The Facts on File Dictionary of Clichés* by Christine Ammer to be sure. Best case scenario: you'll find that your phrase is not a cliché (though "best case scenario" *is* a cliché).

Cover Letter:
Responding to a Job Ad

Thanks to technology, it's easy to find open internships and jobs. The Internet is brimming with job boards that post company vacancies; **monster.com** is a big one. And most companies also post their staffing needs on their own sites. In some cases you will have the option to submit your cover letter and resume online. You'll most likely paste them into fields on a form, or possibly send them as an attachment (only if authorized). Newspaper classified sections still run help-wanted ads too.

Regardless of where you see a job ad, the way to respond to it is similar. **Craft your cover letter so it shows you are what the employer states he or she is looking for.** If the employer wants a "self-starter," meaning a person who doesn't need constant supervision to work, say that you are one (if it's true), but don't repeat the term. Think of an original way to write it. Fill as many of the employer's exact needs as you can, but don't stretch the truth.

Here's how to write an extraordinary cover letter in response to a job advertisement.

Write an opening paragraph that does not resemble the dozens of other letters that will start with a variation on "I am responding to your recent ad in the *Townville Newspaper*." Mention the ad you're responding to, but don't focus on it.

In the second paragraph **describe yourself in a fresh, desirable way.** Don't load up on adjectives. Mention your successes at other jobs and in school, and illustrate at least one of them with a brief, memorable anecdote. Emphasize your positive attitude and your ability to learn.

In the third paragraph (or second, if you don't include two middle paragraphs) **explain why you want to work for the company,** and give concrete examples of ways you will be an asset to the employer.

Keep the final paragraph short and upbeat. End by placing the ball in the employer's court without coming off as pushy. Rather than writing "I hope to hear from you," write with confidence as if you know you will hear from the employer. For example, write "I look forward to hearing from you to arrange an interview."

TIP FILE

Don't repeat your phone number within the body of a cover letter. It's in your header.

EXTRAORDINARY JOB AD COVER LETTER

SCOTT TREMONT
67 HAMBURGER CIRCLE
JEEPERS, NY 67000
(518) 555-1234

June 20, 2006

Jenna Kessler
Food for Thought
902 Yummy Lane
Doughkeepsie, NY 76000

Dear Ms. Kessler:

After years of placing help-wanted ads in the *New York Chronicle*, I recently found myself searching them. Your ad seeking a consultant for your hotel food-supply division stood out.

In 1993 I founded You Can Eat All, the first all-natural catering company in upstate New York. Because of rigorous recipe testing, selective marketing, and a healthy dose of word of mouth, the company grew rapidly. Within six months of starting it, I had more clients than I could handle alone, so I hired an assistant, then another, then a third.

After eight fulfilling years, I felt I had done what I set out to do with my company, and I decided to sell it. Then I took time off to travel the world, sampling a colorful variety of cuisine I'd only dreamed about. Upon my return a week ago, I began to look for a new direction in the food industry—one equally challenging, but without regular late nights. Your company has long impressed me by pushing the hotel industry to offer healthier food. Your ad appealed to me because you want a motivated individual who pays as much attention to his customers as he does to a fine meal. That describes me perfectly. My cooking background combined with my entrepreneurial experience would give me insight into the two main aspects of your business.

Thank you for your time. I welcome the opportunity to meet with you in person to discuss in detail what I could do for your company. I look forward to hearing from you.

Sincerely,

Scott Tremont

Cover Letter:
Applying for a Job by Referral

Networking is a great alternative to combing help-wanted ads. When a relative or friend refers you to someone at a company you would like to work for, you are already validated. A mutual contact who personally endorses you may be the next most beneficial tool you could have, after a strong cover letter and resume.

Here's how to write an extraordinary cover letter for a job you were referred to.

In the first sentence mention the name of the person who referred you and how you know him or her. That will get an employer to read on better than a catchy yet less direct line will.

Keep the second paragraph short and sweet, detailing points about you that would make you attractive to someone looking for this specific job. Be creative. For example, rather than writing that you are good at time management, modestly mention how others have said that about you.

In your closing reiterate that you appreciate this person's time. Don't be presumptuous; even a personal connection won't guarantee that someone is saving a job for you.

TIP FILE

Never use someone's name without obtaining his or her permission first, even if you're sure that person would grant it.

Here's a sample cover letter based on a referral.

EXTRAORDINARY REFERRAL COVER LETTER

ADRIENNE MCCANDLES
50 Ray Road
Enigma, UT 44000
(801) 555-6789

June 20, 2006

Jacob Michaels
Museum of Natural Mystery
900 Sherlock Way
Enigma, UT 11110

Dear Mr. Michaels:

Wendy McCardle referred me to you. Although she has sat in front of me for four years in homeroom, I only recently learned that her uncle works at my favorite museum in town.

As Wendy might have mentioned, I am looking for a position as a tour guide at the museum. I've been there at least once every other month for as long as I can remember, so I can recite the details of the permanent exhibits backwards by now. In school I've taken a liking to public speaking, and classmates have told me I have a knack for it.

If the position is still available and I seem like I might be a potential candidate, I look forward to hearing from you. In the meantime, I will be polishing my magnifying glass.

Thank you,

Adrienne McCandles

Here are a few other ways to add sizzle to a cover-letter opening.

ORDINARY	EXTRAORDINARY
I would like to apply for the job you listed in the newspaper.	Your Web site designer job is only the second job I've applied for in my life. I applied for the first one six years ago, got it, and have worked there happily ever since. I would now like to use the skills I learned there in a new opportunity.
Allow me to introduce myself.	I grew up with two brothers, two sisters, two cats, and two dogs. It seems fitting that I'm now interested in working for a real zoo—yours.
Please find enclosed my resume for consideration.	Enclosed is a tidy summary of my achievements.

EXTRA HELP

Check out *101 Best Cover Letters* by Jay A. Block and Michael Betrus. It's loaded with samples, probably more than you'll ever need.

Thank-You Letter
for an Interview

When an employer grants you an interview, he or she is not doing you a favor. He or she genuinely wants to find the right person for a job. Still, it takes time out of his or her day, and you should acknowledge your appreciation for that with a thank-you letter. An ordinary thank-you letter thanks an employer but does not indicate that the writer wants to work for that company. An extraordinary thank-you letter is grateful but also enthusiastic. It is also a last chance for you to state that you are interested in the job and then to subtly convince the employer you are right for it.

If six people interview for the same job and you're the only one who sends a follow-up thank-you note, you will stand out. It seems many otherwise polite people don't know that they should write a thank-you note to an interviewer. Now you know better.

Though the nature of thank-you notes is personal, keep a professional tone when thanking an interviewer. As always, keep it short. Traditionally, a thank-you note is handwritten. These days, however, an e-mail thank-you is often okay. Any form of thank you is always better than no thank you.

TIP FILE

Send the thank-you note as soon after the interview as you can—ideally the same day. That way the interview is still fresh in your mind when you're writing—and your rapidly received note will keep you fresh in the mind of the interviewer.

How to Say Thank You

From start to finish, here are the steps for writing an extraordinary thank-you letter.

Address the letter formally. If the interviewer asked you to call him or her by his or her first name in person, you may address him or her that way here too.

Openly state that you are interested in the job. Employers appreciate when you're forthright.

Mention specific points discussed in the interview. This shows you were listening, not just talking, and can be used to emphasize what you like about the company.

If applicable, provide a memorable detail about the interview in case you are not the only person who met with the employer.

If it feels right, **compliment the company.**

Some books suggest that you offer to answer any additional questions, but that is probably not necessary. Any employer who is left with questions will ask them even if you don't offer, so don't devote space to it.

Make your closing short and poised. Take the opportunity to reiterate your desire to get the job, and do so in a refined way.

Here's a sample thank-you letter for an interview.

EXTRAORDINARY THANK-YOU LETTER

SHANIQUA ROGERS
712 RAMBLING WAY
LAWLIN, KY 50505
(502) 555-1234

September 15, 2007

Dear Mr. Dovatelli,

Thank you again for meeting with me on June 6 regarding the paralegal position. I'm even more interested in it now that I've had the chance to talk with you. I was especially intrigued by your thoughts on cyberlaw and your firm's reputation in that regard.

I was also pleased to learn that every paralegal is assigned a lawyer with whom they have lunch once a week. That personal guidance shows your dedication to "raising" good lawyers. I happened to speak with one of your paralegals on my elevator ride down, and he said the mentor lunch hour is more valuable than a week's worth of studying!

I look forward to the possibility of working together.

Sincerely,

Shaniqua Rogers

Here are a few other ways to invigorate your interview thank-you letter.

ORDINARY	EXTRAORDINARY
I appreciate your time.	I appreciate your time, even more so now that I see how busy the office is.
I look forward to hearing from you.	I'm hoping the next time we meet is my first day on the job.
I would like to work for you.	I am confident I would make a valuable contribution to your company.

Resolving a
Customer Complaint Letter

Okay, you've got the job. And you still have to write letters? Yes—and don't say you weren't warned. One type of letter some people must write on the job is a "fix it" letter. Companies that truly value their customers send these kinds of letters in response to customers who are unhappy with a product or service.

In school you may be assigned to write a practice "fix it" letter relevant to your school or city. It's a good way to challenge your ability to be nice to someone who may not be! For example, you could pretend you are a city official who must write a letter to a citizen who has complained that the sidewalks in his neighborhood are cracking.

The three essentials of a "fix it" letter are the following:

1. Be civil no matter how aggressive a customer was.

2. If your company is to blame for the problem, own up to it and rectify it promptly.

3. If your company is not to blame, say so politely but still rectify it promptly.

TIP FILE

"Fix it" letters are opportunities in disguise. A company can turn a negative into a positive by listening to its customers' gripes and acting on them.

Fix It Letters

Ready to try your hand at the "fix it" letter?
The following suggestions will help you make yours
exceptional.

**Apologize on behalf of your company, even if
you're not actually at fault.** A sentence is enough to
do it. Just state you're sorry in plain language and move
on to what you can do to calm the customer.

**Offer whatever your company can to pacify the
person** writing the letter, and do it without passing
judgment. In other words, just as you don't need to
accept blame, you shouldn't blame the customer,
either. This may cost the company a little bit of money,
but it's worth it to avoid losing a customer.

**Maintain an unemotional tone throughout the let-
ter.** Resist becoming defensive. Use a gracious closing
paragraph or sentence, reminding the customer that
you appreciate his or her business.

Here's a sample "fix it" letter.

EXTRAORDINARY "FIX IT" LETTER

THEO PALMER
PUPS AND DOWNS
81 JORDAN AVENUE, SUITE 5
NORTH WOODS, WI 12399
(414) 555-4321

June 30, 2006

Hannah Brothers
765 Ninth Street
Allgood, RI 90173

Dear Ms. Brothers:

Thank you for purchasing our Hot Dog Collar for your puppy, Fuzzball. On behalf of Pups and Downs, we are sorry to hear that Fuzzball did not seem to like the product. Furthermore, we are sorry that it was not clear from the name and packaging that the collar is indeed shaped like a hot dog.

Our customers are our top priority. We will be happy to send you a full refund for the collar or another product of equal or lesser value. Please return the collar to my attention at the address on this stationery, and let me know which you prefer. We will respond promptly.

If you have any additional questions or concerns, please call or e-mail me. We are confident that Fuzzball will enjoy whatever substitute you choose for him and hope that you will continue to be a Pups and Downs customer.

Sincerely,

Theo Palmer
Customer Service Representative
Pups and Downs

SAMPLE LETTER

Letter of Recommendation

In a previous section you read how helpful a referral can be in business. At some point you may not be the one using a referral but writing one. **A letter of recommendation is written by an employer about an employee who is applying for another job.** It can also be written by a colleague instead of a boss. And it's an honor to be asked to write one. The credibility of any letter of recommendation begins with the credibility of the writer.

You'll also probably have to write a letter of recommendation or two in school. Some colleges ask for peer recommendations with applications, as do some scholarships and summer programs. Also, in a class on public speaking, you may be assigned to give a speech about a classmate (sometimes called an introductory speech), and the skills you'll pick up here will help you with that as well.

You may have one of these two common concerns when someone asks you to write a letter of recommendation for a job:

- you don't know the person well

- you don't like the person

In the first case, feel free to set up a brief meeting with that person so you can learn enough about him or her to write a recommendation. In the second case, you may politely decline. If you can't write with genuine enthusiasm about him or her, it might show, and that wouldn't do him or her any good anyway. Explain to the person who asked you to write a letter of recommendation that you feel he or she can surely find someone more qualified. However, you may write the letter and be honest, describing the person as a less than ideal candidate.

People asking for letters of recommendation generally have a choice as to whether they get a copy of the letter. If they choose to get a copy, the letter loses value; the person reading it might assume the writer was not completely honest because he or she knew the person the letter is about would read it. Therefore, letters of recommendation are more valuable when the person the letter is about does not request a copy.

When writing a letter of recommendation, overcome the impulse to cram in adjectives. You are aiming to illustrate someone's skills by evaluating tasks he or she has done well. This will come across more vibrantly if you think narratively—in effect, if you relate one or two anecdotes about the person that demonstrate how he or she achieved positive results.

"Don't say it was 'delightful'; make us say 'delightful' when we've read the description. You see, all those words (horrifying, wonderful, hideous, exquisite) are only like saying to your readers 'Please will you do the job for me.'"
—C. S. Lewis (1898–1963)

Sample Descriptions

You want to be clear, specific, but not too flowery when writing a recommendation.

Take a look at how you can transform the descriptions in your letter.

ORDINARY	EXTRAORDINARY
hard worker	skilled problem-solver
dedicated employee	a constant source of ideas and has a strong commitment to the needs of the organization
meets deadlines	finishes projects on time, if not ahead of time
works well with people	provides support and guidance to her staff and handles clients with her strong diplomatic skills

MORE RECOMMENDATIONS

There are a number of sites that offer tips and samples of recommendation letters for you to check out.

On the monster.com site, there are sample letters and paragraph-by-paragraph instructions:
http://resume.monster.com/articles/recommendation/

At the Quintessential Careers site, there is an article with pointers and tips on recommendation letters:
http://www.quintcareers.com/recommendation_letters.html

Writing Recommendations

Here's how to write an extraordinary letter of recommendation.

If you haven't been given a name to whom you should address the letter, a useful salutation is "Good morning."

Write about the person in a professional context, but also comment on him or her personally. That gives the letter a greater sense of authenticity.

If you mention the person's job, **summarize his or her job responsibilities** in case the person reading the letter does not know much about that particular job.

Convey the person's depth of character by relating an anecdote that shows him or her in the best light.

Show rather than tell. Instead of describing a person as "dedicated," give an example of something he or she did that demonstrates his or her dedication. For example, perhaps he or she was the first person at work every day.

Any recommendation should close with your final word on the person. Do you recommend him or her without reservation, with some reservation, or not at all?

Here's a sample letter of recommendation.

EXTRAORDINARY **LETTER OF RECOMMENDATION**

AMIR BARASHKA
Aquatropics Resort
1200 Palm Tree Lane
Foreverglades, FL 38888
(305) 555-6789

October 25, 2006

Subject: Letter of Recommendation for Ms. Olivia Queen

Good morning,

By my own estimate, I've written about thirty letters of recommendation in my career. None have been as easy—or bittersweet—as this one.

good job summary

Olivia has worked under my supervision as an event planner at the Aquatropics Resort for more than five years. She began as an assistant and quickly rose to become our most requested planner in a department of eight. Her responsibilities include meeting with clients who wish to host an event at our resort, helping them determine the nature of their event, and guiding them through every step of the planning. She has run more than twenty events in the last two years, almost one a month. They range from small board meetings to celebrity birthday parties with two hundred attendees.

When the pressure's on, Olivia remains focused. Her relaxed demeanor has calmed many stressed individuals when unforeseen problems arose. Since we're in Florida, hurricanes tend to spoil events—or threaten to spoil them—several times a year. As one storm began, Olivia once single-handedly moved one hundred chairs indoors from the lawn for a wedding while her staff was handling another emergency. She ruined her dress and scraped her arms, but never complained. It was her pleasure to help make the event go off as well as she could. She didn't even want the couple to know she had done it without help, because she knew they would feel bad.

I recommend Olivia without hesitation for any position requiring a level head, a mind for logistics, and a generous spirit. The finest moments of her career are surely yet to come. We will be sorry to see her go, and you will be lucky to have her. If she grows restless there, please send her back!

clear statement of recommendation

Sincerely,

Amir Barashka
Vice President, Special Events

Sales Letter

We are all salespeople. At some point we all want to get someone to see our point of view or to buy what we're selling. In school you may have to write the equivalent of a sales letter, even if it doesn't resemble a sales letter from the business world. Say you're producing a school play and you want to write a letter to parents asking them to take out an ad in the program to help pay for the play. Or perhaps you have to write a persuasive essay. That, believe it or not, is a form of sales letter! (Your topic might be trying to persuade young people to do something, such as open a savings account or volunteer for community service.)

An ordinary sales letter explains what you're selling but doesn't make it sound irresistible and doesn't encourage the reader to act immediately. **An extraordinary sales letter hypes what you're selling in a way that compels the reader to act immediately**. It must be energetic but not so much that it turns off the reader. It explains why what you're selling is better than any competition, or why your offer is too valuable to ignore.

The mission of any sales letter is to make a product or service seem indispensable to a targeted group. You're not going to try to sell bikinis to men or earmuffs to Hawaiians. Know your audience to have maximum effect. In school if you're writing to fellow teens, write to them in a style that teens respond to. If you're writing to parents, you'll have to adopt a different tone. No matter who your audience is, you have lots of creative freedom when writing an extraordinary sales letter.

Once you're in the workforce, you'll find that all companies share a common goal: making a profit. Some sales letters are sent from one business to another. Others are sent directly to consumers. Either way, if you can write a persuasive one, you will be a prized commodity in the business world. Your talent leads directly to higher revenues!

Before the marketing of a new product begins, the company needs to identify who is going to use it. In the chart below, we have listed two types of people who might be interested in it.

PRODUCT	GROUP 1	GROUP 2
MP3 player	parents of teenagers	college students
mountain bike	health enthusiasts	messengers
breath mints	people with halitosis	young professionals
disposable (single-use) camera	people going on vacation	teenagers

Who do you think are the target groups for low-carb ice cream, camera cell phones, or e-books? Once you know who is likely to use the product, you can tailor your sales letter to meet their needs.

Here's how to write an extraordinary sales letter.

Kick off your letter with a devilishly good teaser. The shorter it is, the greater the chance people will read it. And the more tantalizing it is, the greater the chance that they'll read beyond it. It must be related to what you're selling. It can't be a statement with pure shock value, because the recipient will feel manipulated and toss your letter into the trash. For example, don't write "Free money!" and then start the next paragraph with "We don't offer that. But we do offer ultra-absorbent paper towels. . . ."

Make your pitch. Put yourself in the recipient's position. What could somebody say to you that would convince you to buy what he or she is selling? Don't exaggerate. People want the truth, told in a vibrant way.

Don't clutter the letter with dense explanations or industry-specific mumbo-jumbo. Cut anything that won't enhance what you're selling.

Close with a call to action. Encourage the recipient to take advantage of what you're selling immediately because the opportunity won't last forever (only say it more creatively).

Below is a sample sales letter from a company that makes all-natural skin-care products to a woman who has bought a variety of skin-care products in the past.

EXTRAORDINARY SALES LETTER

Julio Diaz

Satin Silk Skin
24 Willoughby Road
New London, NH 86420
(603) 555-0234

September 4, 2006

Molly Vance
331 Oblong Terrace
Rollings, VA 00600

Dear Ms. Vance,

Here are three reasons to try our all-natural, affordable skin-care products:

Helen of Troy. Cleopatra. Lady Godiva.

They're some of the most exotic women in history, and they didn't have skin-care products with artificial ingredients. If these women were as alluring as the legends claim, it was primarily thanks to natural oils, herbs, clays, and extracts.

Life may be more complicated now, but skin care doesn't have to be. Like our fabled ancestors, both real and mythical, Satin Silk Skin knows that the secret to beautiful skin is hidden in the world around us. We don't just believe it—we go out, find it, bottle it, and bring it to you.

EXTRAORDINARY SALES LETTER

Our promises to our loyal customers:

- We choose ingredients only of the highest quality, many of which we grow ourselves.
- We include ingredients first and foremost for their health benefits, even if the side effects are equally wonderful (example: essential oils are not only wonderful on the skin, but they smell heavenly too).
- We actively promote organic farming.
- We are committed to helping people who value health for themselves and our planet.

We don't promise looks that can launch a thousand ships or charisma that can inspire Shakespearean plays. However, we've found our customers are happy with radiant and healthy skin. We hope you'll soon discover for yourself how they feel.

Two ways to save! From now through March 1, we're happy to offer you a 20 percent discount on any product you purchase and a $50 shopping spree on our site for anyone you refer to us who places an order for $50 or more by March 1.

Sincerely,

Julio Diaz

Sizzling Sample Sales Letter Openings

ORDINARY	EXTRAORDINARY
Our pain reliever works incredibly fast.	Our pain reliever often starts to work faster than it will take for you to read this letter.
We're proud to announce the grand opening of our first store in Northville.	We've put love, time, and hard work into our new store about to open in Northville. All we haven't put into it yet is customers.
Don't you want to take piano lessons from someone who loves teaching?	My fingers are typing this letter, but they'd rather be playing piano.

WANT MORE SAMPLES?

The Write Express site, **http://www.writeexpress.com/ sample-business-letters.html,** contains sample letters and articles about various types of business letters.

PROJECT JUMP START

 Write a sales letter with a twist. Write a listing to sell an item on ebay.com, the auction site. Choose something you own that you are ready to part with (though you won't really be going through with the posting and selling part of this). Write a description of it that makes it sound extraordinarily appealing. Check current auctions for similar items to get ideas, but make your pitch your own. Before including any facts, ask what purpose each fact serves. Why will this piece of information make my item attractive to someone?

Write a letter of recommendation for a friend who is applying for an internship. Even if you don't have a friend applying for an internship, act as though you do and sell the company on him or her in grand style. Tell a colorful story about your friend that makes him or her seem like the kind of person they'd like to be around for a while. Use your knowledge of your friend to evaluate how he or she would be as a colleague. It's often a lot easier to boast when you're doing it on someone else's behalf.

BRAIN JAM:
Facts and Phrases

Find fun facts about yourself. If you have a resume, what are three cool things about you that don't appear on it? Don't think in terms of things you've done but rather things you are. Are you as punctual as a cell-phone bill? Are you the one your friends come to for advice? Are you a person who always finds the good in others? See if you can work your three things into a cover letter in a natural way without being flip or glib.

Getting the words right. With any cover letter, if you currently have a job and want a delicate way to explain why you're seeking new employment, a handy phrase is, "I am not being used to my full potential." Can you come up with two other phrases to convey this?

School Activities

The local a

Personal Photo

conversations

albums

Mu

paintings

Family stori

CHAPTER 5

DEVELOPING
HIGH-IMPACT RESUMES

Your One-Page
Autobiography

Developing High-Impact Resumes

The average employer receives hundreds of resumes a week and scans each one for sixty seconds or less. The employer evaluates your worth in one minute. Make every word count. Sometimes it's easy to determine what to include in your resume. What can be difficult is determining what to leave out.

Essentially, every resume has the same ingredients. They're just mixed differently for each person. A resume is not about fanciness. It's a straightforward summary of your qualifications.

There are countless ways to format your resume, but here are a few standards. The resume of people starting out in the workforce should be one page long. It should be typed on white, $8\frac{1}{2}$-by-11-inch paper. Mark each section header clearly, either in bold, all capital letters, or both. Leave a blank line between each section to further separate them. Use only one or two fonts at the most, both size 12. If you want to use two fonts, try using one font for your name, contact information, and the section headers (Education, Experience, and so on), and another font for everything else. For consistency, use the font (or one of the two fonts) in your resume as the font of your cover letter. Choose a businesslike font.

Times New Roman, Arial, Helvetica, or Courier are recommended. Alleycat, STENCIL, FAJITA, and Curlz are most definitely not.

BASIC RESUME BLUEPRINT

Name

Address/Home Phone Number/E-mail Address

OBJECTIVE OR PROFILE

EXPERIENCE

EDUCATION

SKILLS

AWARDS/HONORS

ACTIVITIES

INTERESTS/HOBBIES

make
name
large

run
contact
info on
one line

make
section
names
stand
out

keep
resume
to one
page

Your resume header will not be the word "resume." It will be your name as you would like it to appear professionally. Center your name at the top of the page. Immediately below your name, include your contact information. This includes your full mailing address, telephone number (sometimes both home and cell), e-mail address, and perhaps Web site URL if it looks professional and relates to the job you're applying for. To conserve space, write your contact information across one line rather than putting each element on a separate line. Don't write "address" before your address, "telephone" before your number, or "e-mail" before your e-mail address.

Many resumes are divided into two main sections: your relevant work experience and your relevant education. Once you graduate from college, you typically won't include your education prior to college.

Many resumes include a section outlining your relevant skills, such as the software you know how to use and the languages besides English you can speak and write. An employer can't always tell these things from your education and work experience, or you may have marketable skills that you haven't yet used on a job.

Close with a somewhat personal section listing your volunteer work, community activities, and personal interests.

Don't use complete sentences on your resume. It's acceptable to skip the personal pronouns "I" and "my" and articles such as "the" and "a." They slow down the flow of reading.

Resume Extras

Here are three more items you may find on a resume:

An objective. This one- to three-line phrase tells what kind of job you want, what skills you'd bring to it, and what results you are capable of achieving. Some people convey their objectives in cover letters instead of their resumes. That frees up more space on the resume for vital information that wouldn't quite belong in the cover letter.

A profile. This is a short snapshot-in-words of you, used to emphasize your strengths and expertise.

The phrase "References available upon request," often used to close the resume. Among professionals, however, this is implied, so you don't need to write it. If the employer wants to read what others have written about you, he or she will ask. And since you want the job, you'll have them ready.

TIP FILE

It's not necessary to write USA in your address if you're sending your resume within the United States, but it's okay if you want to. And definitely include it if you send your resume internationally.

Tackling Objectives

If you decide to include an objective, place it after your contact information and before your Education and Experience sections. Be as specific as possible.

ORDINARY	EXTRAORDINARY
A challenging position at an environmental company	A position in the fundraising division of an environmental company to assist in planning innovative events that build public awareness of the company's mission.
To work in the fashion industry to expand on my current skills	A marketing position at a fashion company in which I can use my experience creating award-winning print advertisements to increase the exposure of its new brands
Any job that will keep me out of trouble	An engineering position at an electronic toy company that requires strong problem-solving skills and knowledge of the technical realities of product design for children

Tackling Profiles

Pretend you bump into the boss of your dreams in an elevator and have ten floors to sell him or her on you. How would you describe yourself in those twenty seconds so you sound fantastically employable? Your answer would be tailored to your industry, but here's a general one to get you thinking about how you can do it.

SAMPLE PROFILE

> Motivated, reliable critical thinker with more than ten years' experience in the athletic shoe industry solving client problems with courtesy and speed. Boosted morale of staff with positive attitude and open lines of communication. Only person in my department to receive a promotion three years in a row.

A profile gives you the freedom to pat yourself on the back in a way that no other resume section will. Brag well to bag a job. And you *have* to brag about yourself when job searching because no one else is able to do it for you. Remember, employers expect you to! They want someone confident, not someone afraid of saying what's good about himself or herself. If you feel uncomfortable hyping your own accomplishments, privately pretend you're describing a friend.

LEARN FROM THE PROS

These sites feature dozens of robust resume samples for various industries:

- Monster.com sample resumes
  http://resume.monster.com/archives/samples/

- About.com sample resumes
  **http://jobsearch.about.com/od/
  sampleresumes/a/sampleresume2.htm**

Resume:
Work Experience Section

Employers want to know what you've done for others to get an idea of what you can do for them. For each job or internship you put on your resume, include the following:

- name of the company (usually in all caps)

- city and state (or city and country, if not in the United States) of the company

- name of the title(s) you held there

- dates you worked there (for example, April 2005–January 2006; if you still work at a company, indicate it like this: April 2005–present)

- summary of your responsibilities there

- summary of your achievements there

Start off with your most recent job, then continue in reverse chronological order. (It's the closest you'll ever come to traveling back in time.) Leave off your earliest jobs, especially if they're unrelated to the job for which you're applying. Space permitting, put in a brief line or phrase about each company in case an employer isn't familiar with it. Place this directly after the company's name or incorporate it into the first line of your responsibilities and achievements.

What if you haven't had a "real" job? Don't worry. Getting paid is not what makes something a job. Having responsibility is. Therefore, include anything you've done that shows you're reliable. Babysitting counts. Tutoring counts. Helping out your parents at their places of business counts. Focus on your skills no matter where you used them. You can even list your skills and give examples of where you've used each of them.

Your resume is a writing sample and should be written with flair. Your goal is to be both accurate and intriguing. Describe your responsibilities and achievements in a rapid-fire collection of muscular, punchy phrases. Resist any temptation to use more than an occasional adjective, because adjectives are subjective. Instead, pack in facts and figures. You're at an advantage if you can state what you did at the company and then briefly explain how that benefited the company. By spelling out how you solved problems at a previous job, you're suggesting to whomever is reading your resume that you can do the same at his or her company.

Start each phrase on your resume with an action verb. Action verbs energize your resume. Use the past tense consistently (except for the job you still hold, if applicable).

Here are some examples of work experience phrases.

ORDINARY	EXTRAORDINARY
• was responsible for making accounting procedures less labor-intensive	• streamlined accounting procedures, leading to 50 percent greater efficiency
• brought out new software and was in charge of getting the word out	• launched new software and co-chaired six-person promotional team leading to more than 200,000 units in sales
• was responsible for decreasing tenant dissatisfaction by getting rid of housing problems	• began campaign to increase tenant satisfaction by improving housing conditions

If possible, don't repeat any action verbs. Be careful not to exaggerate. Avoid using action verbs with violent connotations. For example, don't claim that your sales strategies "demolished" all expectations or that your ideas "killed" in the marketplace. These words may feel natural in casual conversation, but they come across as aggressive on a resume.

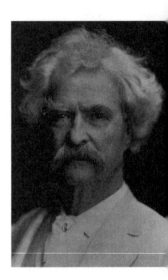

"The difference between the right word and the almost right word is the difference between lightning and lightning-bug."
—Mark Twain (1835–1910)

TIP FILE

Think of ten more action verbs that might pop on a resume. If you get stuck, don't look at other resumes. Instead, read a few articles in the business section of a newspaper or a business magazine. Make note of the verbs used in them.

Try to incorporate at least ten action verbs in your resume. In addition to the verbs above, here are just a few of the many that work well.

- analyzed
- assembled
- changed
- conducted
- coordinated
- counseled
- created
- demonstrated
- designed
- directed
- discovered
- established
- evaluated
- exceeded
- executed
- expanded
- formed
- founded
- generated
- guided
- implemented
- initiated
- maintained
- marketed
- maximized
- minimized
- motivated
- negotiated
- operated
- planned
- presented
- prevented
- produced
- publicized
- recruited
- reported
- researched
- resolved
- restructured
- reviewed
- selected
- served
- shaped
- simplified
- solved
- supervised
- tested
- trained

Visually, using a bulleted list to organize your responsibilities for each job works well, but if that takes up too much space, arrange your points as a paragraph (see the sample entries on the right). Either way, prioritize the information from most impressive to average, and don't attempt to squeeze in every detail from every job—just the most notable. Omit duties you don't wish to do again at future jobs. Don't include results that are underwhelming.

Because of these resume requirements, you might be feeling that there's little room for creativity when crafting yours. Though the contents of professional resumes tend to follow certain patterns, you have a world of options in the way you write the contents. That's where the creativity comes into play. That's where you have tremendous potential to shine.

TIP FILE

Load your resume with key words specific to your industry, especially if the resume will be posted on the Web. These are words that an employer may use to search online for a job candidate. The more key words you have that they want, the better shot you have at landing an interview. For example, if you're looking for a position in computer technical support, list the computer programs you know, such as Java, HTML, C++, and so on.

Work Experience Entries

ORDINARY	EXTRAORDINARY
THE CHASM, Bethem, KY	THE CHASM, Bethem, KY
Employee	Assistant Manager
June 2005–present	June 2005–present
I handled things in the store when the manager was not present. When she was present, I assisted her. My duties included greeting customers, ringing up sales, cleaning the back room, shelving merchandise, and closing up.	Ran all aspects of retail clothing chain underneath head manager. Conceived Back-to-School promotion that spiked sales 40 percent in August and September. Redecorated store windows every three weeks to draw foot traffic. Informed customers of products similar to what they were purchasing, leading to a 20 percent increase in per-customer sales, on average. Greeted and rang up customers.
STIPPLE BOOKS, INC., New York, NY	STIPPLE BOOKS, INC., New York, NY Leader in high-quality book publishing since 1951, now with $22 million in annual revenue.
Assistant (November 2004-September 2006)	Marketing Assistant (November 2004–September 2006)
Wrote marketing materials. Helped choose new products. Wrote ads announcing book events. Helped build e-mail newsletter subscriber list.	Composed direct-mail campaign for new series of biography books that yielded a 60 percent response rate. Consulted CEO on acquisitions for children's book line, including picture book that won prestigious Hey, That's Good award. Wrote promotional copy for advertisements announcing book signings. Developed and authored monthly e-mail newsletter and increased subscriber base from 350 to 750 customers. Strengthened customer relations by checking in with a different one every day, even when they had not voiced a concern.

Resume: Education Section

If you are in high school you should state what school you attend, your GPA if it's impressive, and any academic awards or honors you've received. Since school is still the focus of your life, you might consider putting your education section above your experience section. Otherwise, in the short term, put first whichever section is stronger. After you've had at least one major job, it's probably better to begin a resume by putting your work experience first.

These are the key facts to list in the education section:

- name of your high school or university (usually in all caps)

- city and state (or city and country, if not in the United States) of the university or high school

- name of the degree(s) you earned or will earn there

- year you graduated or will graduate

- achievements, honors, and awards (could include advanced-placement classes, a strong GPA, honor-society memberships, academic distinctions such as summa cum laude, speeches you've been asked to give, and anything else applicable)

- notable extracurricular activities

"Technique is only a telephone wire—what's important is the message going through it."
—Kent Nagano (1951–)

That may seem like a lot, but it all can fit in a few lines. Look at this example:

SAMPLE EDUCATION SECTION

EDUCATION
SIEGEL HIGH SCHOOL, Cleveland, OH
Graduation date: May 2008. GPA 3.4.
Top 10 percent of class.

Honors: Member, National Honor Society. Cleveland Creative Arts Scholarship recipient.

Activities: Member of soccer team freshman, sophomore, junior years. Created and served as president of Gay/Straight Unity Club.

As with work experience, list your most recent schooling first, then continue in reverse chronological order. If you hit kindergarten, you've gone way too far.

Resume: Skills Section

Include which computer platforms you know how to use (PC, Macintosh, or both). List all the mainstream computer software you know how to use if it's not already part of your work experience (again, use key words).

List any languages besides English in which you are fluent or proficient, but only if you'd like to use these languages in a work environment. For some jobs foreign language experience is a major asset.

List any special equipment you know how to use, such as a cash register. Skills can also include qualities you possess, such as attention to detail or good customer service skills. If you're stuck trying to summarize these kinds of skills, use your activities to help you find them.

For example, if you've run a school fund-raising event, that indicates you have leadership, organizational, and financial skills. If you were on the yearbook design committee, that shows your ability to work in a team and your ability to meet deadlines. **If you're still stuck,** ask a friend what he or she thinks your best qualities are. Would any of them be desirable to a potential employer?

SKILLS
Proficient in Microsoft Word and PowerPoint; fluent in Spanish; experienced cash register operator; stickler for detail; strong leadership, organizational, and financial skills.

If you have other skills desirable to your industry that don't turn up elsewhere in your resume, here's your chance to trumpet them. For example, if you're applying for a position at a dude ranch, the cowboys and cowgirls doing the hiring would be thrilled to see that you know how to lasso a runaway calf while riding a horse.

Volunteer Work, Community Activities, and Personal Interests Section

Unless anything in this section takes up every waking hour when you're not at school or work, you should be able to encapsulate everything here in a line or three. Here's an example.

SAMPLE ACTIVITIES SECTION

ACTIVITIES
Volunteer at an afterschool program every Wednesday; participate annually in the Multiple Sclerosis Walk

INTERESTS
Swimming, Asian cooking, collecting silent-movie posters

Don't underestimate the potential influence of your hobbies. It's your brief moment to introduce your personal side. Maybe nothing else on your resume resonated with an employer until he or she saw that you are a space fanatic, just like he or she is. If the rest of your resume is nonetheless solid, you might get an interview based on the cosmic connection alone!

If you do rattle off your interests, take advantage of the fact that they will be the last thing a potential employer reads. End with a kicker—something unusual for a resume, but still true to you. If the rest of your resume is the peak of professionalism, you can get away with adding a little spice.

TIP FILE

A word about lying on your resume: don't. It will come back to humiliate you one day. What if you just change a few dates so it looks like there are no gaps in your employment history? Or if you make your title "manager" instead of "assistant"? Will they really check? Do you want to explain yourself if they do? So again: Don't lie.

Paperless Resumes

Since the World has gotten its Wide Web, many employers now prefer that you e-mail your resume to them or post it online for them to view. However, do that only if an employer offers it, and follow its directions. Some will allow you to attach your resume to an e-mail, while others may request that you paste the text into the body of an e-mail.

Whether you paste or post, you're best off converting your resume to a format called ASCII (pronounced "as-key") beforehand. Different computer platforms "read" files differently, but every computer is supposed to be able to read ASCII, otherwise known as "plain text" or "text only." You want your formatting to remain intact no matter where it zips to through cyberspace, and ASCII is the way to do it. To be sure your resume will transfer properly, even in ASCII, always e-mail it to yourself first to test it.

In terms of design, all ASCII resumes look the same— no frills. **Don't boldface, italicize, or underline words.** Get rid of lines separating sections. Instead of those cool dot or square bullets, go with asterisks or hyphens. A resume that contains special formatting may get messed up on someone else's system. Also, some employers' computer systems automatically scan all resumes they receive electronically, and again, fancy formatting may go berserk in the process.

No one expects electronic resumes to be works of art, so don't be embarrassed if yours does not look flashy. In this case a simple layout will only make yours look more professional.

TIP FILE

Here's how to save your file in ASCII in many word processing programs:

1. Select the "Save As" command from the File menu.
2. A window will open. Choose the "Text Only with Line Breaks" in the format menu.
3. Click the "Save" button.

Your Resume Will Grow

As you build your career, your resume will grow. You'll need to update it continually, but still keep it to one page, at least until you become such a big shot that you can afford more room.

Once you've finalized your first resume, save it as "resume 1." Then, whenever you open it to modify it, immediately rename it "resume 2," and so on. That way you'll maintain a record of every version of your resume. If you ever want to restore something you once deleted—or just take a visual stroll down resume lane—you'll be able to.

Sample Resume

This resume synthesizes what you just learned. It is just one possible layout of many. Experiment with yours to maximize the information you provide without crowding the page.

Jeremy is a music lover who is seeking a new position in the music industry. See how the use of two columns— one for dates of employment and name of company and the other for the responsibilities and achievements— uses space wisely? See how Jeremy has only two prior jobs (the most recent of which is surely unpaid) but makes them look stupendous? If it makes you look good and fits on one page, put it in.

JEREMY STANTON

1 First Avenue • Blue Bay, NY 10000 • USA • 212-555-0000 • jstanton@pleaseemail.com

OBJECTIVE

An internship at a growing record label where I can apply my organizational skills while gaining insight into the creative side of the music industry. Possess tireless work ethic and lifelong love of rock and roll.

EXPERIENCE

INTERN
The Music Maze
Browntown, PA
September 2005–
present

Perform various administrative and technical duties at this recording studio. Manage the booking schedule for the recording studios. Give band members tours of the studio to encourage them to record with us. Set up audio equipment before each band session. Accompany studio director to local trade shows to assist in making decisions about what new equipment to purchase.

CUSTOMER
REPRESENTATIVE
Stan Goodly Music
Violetville, PA
September 2003–
June 2005

Assisted customers in their music and movie selections at this chain store. Manned cashier. Assisted in opening and closing store. Stocked shelves with new releases. Stayed informed about the music industry by reading *Sing Me a Song* magazine every month.

EDUCATION

Zale High School
North Haven, CT

A senior who will graduate in May 2007. GPA 3.7. Class rank 16 out of 345. Taking advanced placement calculus and English. Coursework includes music history.

SKILLS

• Can set up and operate most audio recording equipment.
• Computer: Windows, Word, PowerPoint, Internet
• Languages: Spanish (proficient)

AWARDS/HONORS

• Student of the Month, April 2006
• Music for Life Scholarship recipient, 2007
• Have played guitar since age 6

**EXTRACURRICULAR
ACTIVITIES**

• Write music-review column for school newspaper
• Volunteer at soup kitchen two Sundays a month

INTERESTS

learning piano, basketball, singing (only when alone in the car)

PROJECT JUMP START

★ **Write your resume in reverse chronological order.** Focus on your experience, both school and work, in reverse order. (That means list the most recent first.)

★ **Write a second version of your reverse chronological resume geared toward a different type of company than the first.** For example, say your top two passions are cinema and gardening. If your first resume is designed to get you an internship at a movie studio, try writing one that is geared toward landing a position at a gardening center. Some information will overlap with the first one, but it will have to be presented it in a different way. Experiment. Vary the action verbs. Rearrange the order of your achievements. Maybe you'll end up getting both jobs.

BRAIN JAM:
Get Resume Ready

Write your twenty-second biography. That means it should take twenty seconds for someone to read. That's shorter than your resume will be! What are the key events in your life? Don't think solely in terms of internships or jobs you've held. Think about the top six to ten moments in your life. Make a short list. Each moment should be a single line. This exercise will start to expose you to the nature of resume writing. You may even be able to transfer some of these moments to your resume.

Write an objective for your dream job. It must be short, yet still contain three elements: what kind of job you want, what skills you have, and how you can benefit the company.

Ask to see your parents' resumes. Hunt down and circle any passive verb constructions at the start of phrases. Tell your parents what you've learned, and show them what you've found. You'll be helping them take their resumes from ordinary to extraordinary.

TO FIND OUT MORE

Books

Begun, Ruth Weltmann, ed. *Ready-to-Use Social Skills Lessons & Activities for Grades 7–12*. Hoboken, NJ: Jossey-Bass, 2002.

Bell, Arthur H. *Writing Effective Letters, Memos, & E-mails*. Hauppauge, NY: Barron's Educational Series, 2004.

Bond, Alan. *Over 300 Successful Business Letters for All Occasions*. Hauppauge, NY: Barron's Educational Series, 1998.

Danziger, Elizabeth. *Get to the Point! Painless Advice for Writing Memos, Letters and E-mails Your Colleagues and Clients Will Understand*. New York: Three Rivers Press, 2001.

Goldsmith, Andrew. *One Hour Wiz: Landing Your First Job—The Legendary, World Famous Method to Interviewing, Finding the Right Career Opportunity and Landing Your First Job*. Boston: Aspatore Books, 2001.

Greene, Brenda. *Get the Interview Every Time: Fortune 500 Hiring Professionals' Tips for Writing Winning Resumes and Cover Letters*. Chicago: Dearborn Trade, 2004.

Ireland, Susan. *The Complete Idiot's Guide to Cool Jobs for Teens*. New York: Alpha, 2001.

Learning Express. *501 Grammar and Writing Questions, 2nd Edition*. New York: Learning Express, 2002.

Learning Express. *Vocabulary & Spelling Success in 20 Minutes a Day, 3rd Edition*. New York: Learning Express, 2002.

Organizations and Web Sites

Business Letter Writing
http://www.business-letter-writing.com
This site has information on writing business letters
and resources on business writing and job searches.
There is a section that has links to useful directories.

The Guide to Grammar and Writing
http://ccc.commnet.edu/grammar
This site assists students on a variety of writing topics.
It has tips and activities for grammar, sentence, and
paragraph structure.

Resume-Resource.com
http://www.resume-resource.com
This site gives free advice on writing resumes and
cover letters. There are also samples to see and other
related resources.

Writer's Digest
http://www.writersdigest.com
This site is a general resource for writers.

INDEX

MARC TYLER NOBLEMAN

I have written more than fifty books for young readers with publishers including Scholastic, HarperCollins, and Dutton. My titles include *How to Do a Belly Flop*, *365 Adventures*, *5-Minute Daily Practice: Writing*, and *Vocabulary Cartoon of the Day*. I have been a regular contributor of activities, humor, and nonfiction to magazines including *Nickelodeon* and several *Weekly Reader* publications. Also a cartoonist, my single panels have appeared in more that one hundred international publications, including *Wall Street Journal*, *Barron's*, *Forbes*, and *Good Housekeeping*.

Here are my three favorite tips:

1. Use the phrase "4-second question" in e-mail subject lines.

2. In the Interests section of a resume, include one unconventional (but true) personal tendency, such as "simplifying" or "putting myself in someone else's position."

3. When sending business letters, use catalog-sized envelopes instead of #10 envelopes. This way, the correspondence won't have to be folded (which looks better) and might even be opened before other correspondence (since we subconsciously think it's easier than unfolding).